The STORY of CHRISTMAS

Written by **Patricia A. Pingry**

Illustrated by
Rebecca Thornburgh

ideals children's books.
Nashville, Tennessee

Do you know why we give gifts at Christmas?

We give presents because it is

Jesus' birthday.

Long ago, an angel told
Mary she would have a baby
named Jesus.

Mary and her husband, Joseph, were very happy. They had a lot to do to get ready for the baby.

But first, they had to take a long
trip to Bethlehem. Mary rode
a donkey. Joseph walked.

When they got to Bethlehem, many people were there. Mary and Joseph were very tired, but there was no place for them to stay.

They slept on a bed of hay in a
stable with cows and donkeys.
That night, Baby Jesus was born.

Angels told the shepherds,
"Jesus is born! You will find Him

lying in a manger."

Wise men followed a star
to the stable and Baby Jesus.

They brought presents
because they **loved** Him.

We give gifts at Christmas
to show our love.

And we say,
"Happy birthday,
Baby Jesus."